BEYOND THE PAIN

10 Lessons on Love, Life, and Letting Go

MARCI MASON

Beyond the Pain: 10 Lessons on Love, Life, and Letting Go

First Edition, 2015

Lorem Publishing, LLC
320 Springs Way, Suite 450
Brentwood, TN 37027

Library of Congress Cataloging-in-Publication Data

Marci Mason,
Blessed Beyond the Pain:
10 Lessons on Love, Life, and Letting Go
Published by: Lorem Publishing, LLC

ISBN: 978-0-578-14988-2

1. Self Help
2. Personal Growth
3. Motivational

Printed in the United States of America

Note: Readers are advised to consult a professional therapist, counselor, or life coach before making any changes in their lives. The reader assumes all responsibility for the consequences of any actions taken based on the information presented in this book. The information in this book is based on the author's research and experience. Every attempt has been made to ensure that the information is accurate; however, the author cannot accept liability for any errors that may exist. The facts and theories on life, love and relationships are subject to interpretation, and the conclusions and recommendations presented here may not agree with other interpretations.

This book is dedicated to the loves of my life, B and D. Nothing I write will truly express how much I love you both. I am grateful God picked me to be your mother. Because of the both of you, I am inspired to be a better person and to live authentically. You two are the reason I know how to love unselfishly. You two are the reason I wake up to live every day! My life matters because of the both of you. I may not be able to help you with every situation in life, but know there will never be a day when I wouldn't try.

Love you both.

-Mom

Contents

Introduction 1

1 Laying the foundation 5

2 Know your value 17

3 Compromise, but don't settle 27

4 Pursue your purpose. 35

5 Love isn't for sale 45

6 Reality vs. Perception .53

7 The breaking point. 61

8 Know your pretty-point 71

9 Parenting through the pain 79

10 Not everything you lose is a loss. 91

Final thoughts 97

About the Author 101

Special Thanks 103

Acknowledgement

I tried to keep silent, but my purpose wouldn't allow me to. Purpose showed me I could fight even when I was outsized and still come out victorious! I've learned that I can be strong even when I feel physically weak. And I can still give love when people aren't so lovable to me.

-M

Beyond the Pain

Introduction

Pain is a universal human experience. It doesn't discriminate by age, religious beliefs, ethnicity, or social and economic backgrounds. It has multiple roots and causes, and people respond to it in different ways. People can't judge, limit, quantify, or qualify your pain.

I've participated in numerous conversations about physical pain. But, for some reason, there are fewer constructive conversations about emotional, mental, and spiritual pain. It is evident by the number of reported break-ups, divorces, and suicides that these painful situations aren't any less prevalent than physical pain in our society today.

It was because of my own personal experience of pain that I was motivated to write this book, share my lessons, and start these conversations with you. I tried to bury my desire to share, but my purpose wouldn't let me. The goal in writing this book is so that it may be used as a tool to transform women. I have opened up my heart and allowed myself to be transparent. I want to empower others to stop hiding behind their problems in shame, to start facing them openly and honestly, and to boldly pick up the pieces of their lives. Men move forward with praise and blessings, while women are often left scorned and devastated. It's a new day, a new time, and we have a new movement. We as women must face the circumstances put before us and adjust accordingly to be better mothers, better wives, and better women!

Ignoring the pain doesn't fix the problem and can contribute to other issues. Registered Clinical Counselor Sarah Irons, MA, found in her research that what begins as an emotional issue can sometimes become a problem that requires medical intervention. I like painting pictures to help stress the point I am seeking to make. Think about a beautiful garden with all of your favorite flowers that are blooming in season. But then, weeds began to grow in your garden and have the potential to choke out all of the beautiful flowers. Pain in life can be compared to this garden. If we ignore the weeds in the garden, they certainly damage the beauty of the flowers. Life is no different. If we ignore the problems, they have the potential to damage other parts of our lives and even begin to be accepted as the norm. We must be careful not to allow our abnormal situations and circumstances to become so comfortable that we no longer see the need for change. Sometimes, we don't discuss our pain because we are ashamed of our situations. Other times, we may feel like victims of our own circumstances. Discussing it subjects us to truths we just may not be ready to face. But it's when we begin to open up, acknowledge our pain, and exercise our faith to change that we can start the process of moving beyond it. Moving beyond the pain isn't solely about acknowledgement; it also requires taking action. It's about the belief that there is a point beyond what you feel today. It's about assessing your life experiences and making the necessary adjustments to move beyond where you are. Don't you know that if it were easy, everyone would already be doing it?

I hope that my life lessons will resonate with your spirit in a comforting, confirming, and encouraging way. Sometimes, in life, we just need to know there are others who have gone through what we have gone through and have made it. I hope this book will acknowledge those similarities, confirm some truths, and then propel you into some action towards progress and change. You can move beyond the pain. Don't confuse your path with your destination!

Laying the foundation

" The foundation stones for a balanced success are honesty, character, integrity, faith, love and loyalty."

- Zig Ziglar

I HAD DREAMS AND aspirations for my life. I knew just what I wanted to accomplish. I was going to graduate high school, finish college, and get started on building my career path. After establishing my independence and reaching some career goals, I wanted to get married and start my very own family. It sounds like I at least had a plan for my foundation, right? Well, for the most part, I did. I carried myself like a lady as Mom had always instructed me to do. I graduated high school, finished college with a Bachelor's Degree in Finance, and later became one of the youngest purchasing managers for the General Motors Corporation. I was young, on track to meet my goals, and enjoying the zest of life. It was what happened next that would forever change my plans, shape my destiny, and formulate the foundation of my future.

The summer after I graduated college, I went back for a basketball game where a fight broke out, and, as a result of the scatter, I was face-to-face with one of the security guards, who happened to be on crutches. I thought that to be funny; I felt so protected as I was fleeing the gym for my safety. He mentioned to me that I looked nice. I quickly responded with "Thanks" and headed for the door. You know how it is when we are trying to get to safety! My girlfriend later told me that the guy on crutches had inquired to her boyfriend about me on many occasions. I was not ready for a committed relationship and didn't give meeting him much thought at that time. In any event, we had met, and life continued as usual.

Now, let's move forward about six months. My same girlfriend and I had plans to go see the highly anticipated movie *Waiting to Exhale*, featuring Whitney Houston. I threw on some jeans and a top and was ready to hang out with my girl. I drove to her place only to find she was not yet dressed, and our movie was going to start shortly! I was not happy as I hate being late. We decided to see the next showing, and she peddled around as if getting dressed were the absolute hardest thing she'd ever had to do in life. In the midst of waiting for her to get dressed, there was a knock at the door. That was strange. *Who would be coming over when we should be at the movies?* She headed to the door with this mischievous smile on her face. The door opened, and I could see her boyfriend and a shadow of someone behind him. The three of them were looking at me as if they were unsure if their little plan to trick me had worked or really made me angry. I was introduced to this guy who was the good friend of my girl's boyfriend. I felt he looked familiar. I thought, *I know you from the basketball game. This is the guy who had been inquiring about me to my friend. Did my friend just set me up on a blind date without my knowledge?* I didn't know this guy on a personal level, and there was no way I was riding with him alone. Well, my girlfriend decided we would all ride together in their car, making it a double date. I'll never forget that forest green Toyota Camry. It wasn't her boyfriend's car, so I just assumed it belonged to my blind date. I was glad my girlfriend understood. I thought it better to have an angry friend than to risk my safety.

The evening turned out pretty well. Both guys were on their best behavior, and we girls had a really good time. Turns out, Mr. Security Guard on Crutches was an upcoming senior on the football team at Michigan State

University. He was a humble and modest guy, which was refreshing. We spent a lot of time together and got to know each other over the next year. He didn't have much but was very willing to share all that he had. He gave me a flower once and wrote a note that said, "Only one flower today, but one day I will be able to give you the world." Ironically, I had always felt and expressed to him that material things may contribute to happiness but are not the essential cause of happiness, especially for me. I was far more concerned with having his heart, a mutual respect for our love, and his commitment of loyalty as the foundation of our future lives together than material things. I felt that's what he liked about me. Time passed by and we fell in love. He proposed, and I said, "YES!"

Can we agree that the foundation of a house is the most important part of the structure? Durability and strength depend upon the foundation. Even the inner walls that contribute to finishing the rooms are dependent upon the original foundation. So, the analogy between the foundation of a house and that of life and marriage is appropriate for this life lesson. The foundation that you lay will become the base on which everything else thereafter is built upon.

I've learned that having God's values as the guide for our lives is essential to laying a solid foundation and building a healthy, sustainable relationship. Love is a choice that we must make, and if we don't have a firm base rooted in Godly morals, then our choices will have nothing to anchor them as a part of that solid foundation. We are subject to the possibility of making choices based on our fleshly desires instead of our spiritual guidance. And whenever we make selfish choices based solely on our own fleshly desires, someone is likely to get hurt and the foundation will start to crumble.

Allow me to share the importance of connecting with a man who has God at the center of his life and as the foundation of his future. If God isn't the foundation, what type of future does he hold? What code of ethics will be the standard to lead his family? This leaves him open to make choices out of his weaknesses and not out of God's strength. He needs more than himself to lead a household. As women, we're supposed to follow the lead of our husbands, which is why it is vitally important that the lead is credible to the family and its future.

We have to realize as women that we do have influence, but we don't have control over anyone. A person will be who he is and do what he wants. We have to make sure that whom we choose to settle down with can make the right choices even when no one is watching, choices that build upon the foundation and do not further eradicate it.

Take some time and get closer to God for yourself so you'll be able to hear His instructions for your life. It's important that you understand that God intended for a man to lead, but God never intended for a man to lead without first being led by Him. I'm a firm believer in submitting to my husband, but submitting to a man who isn't submitted to God is spiritually dangerous and emotionally irresponsible. Does your man love God? I'm not asking if his mouth says he loves God. Do his *actions* say that he loves God? That's the question you have to ask yourself. Is he a man of integrity? Is he a man of his word? Does he seek clarity and understanding before he makes a decision in his life? If the answer to these questions is "NO," then you have some decisions to make. These questions are all important to answer because the flesh sometimes gets caught up in physical and material attributes instead of spiritual assets. If we only consider physical attributes, money, and material things, we can overlook the true character traits that matter. Keep this in mind as you make decisions about the man that will lead your family and lay the foundation for your future.

I'd like for you to take time to write some things out. I'm a firm believer in making things clear through writing. Please take the time to write some thoughts or notes after you read each chapter. It's time to make a decision to draw closer to God and to make sure that the man you choose to be in your life is on the same path as you in building a solid foundation for your future together. If two people are building a foundation of character, integrity, faith, love, and loyalty, they are better equipped to weather the storms ahead.

What does laying a solid foundation mean to you?

What character traits are important to you?

Are there any character traits that are deal breakers for you?

Does your mate possess any of these deal breaker traits? (REFLECT DEEPLY.)

Know your value

"Strive not to be a success, but rather to be of value."

~ Albert Einstein

I was planning my wedding and preparing to start my life with my new husband. I spent every tangible dime I had on that wedding. I guess we were old-fashioned, so it was the responsibility of the bride and her family to pay for the wedding. I considered it my first of many investments in us. This was my soul mate; I was going to be with this man until death do us part—our promise to each other. I overlooked the fact that his family didn't respect our relationship and he didn't protect me from their blatant disrespect. I just loved him. In my heart of hearts, I felt I was marrying *him*, not his family. Okay, I was wrong. And there were many life lessons from that alone I could expound upon, but I won't; there are far more pressing lessons to deal with.

The NFL draft was upon us during the planning process of our big day. It was April, and our wedding was set for June. Tensions were high as everyone around him was counting on his success, the big payday. Truth be told, due to a recent injury, we weren't sure when he would go in the draft. His stock most certainly dropped, and we were aware of it. Our life plans certainly were not dependent solely upon the draft. I honestly felt it was this whole NFL possibility that drove the emotions of many to feel he should not get married. But our foundation had already begun to be laid and had nothing to do with football. We loved each other. We wanted to be there to support each other's passions and dreams. We had made the decision to spend the rest of our lives together as husband and wife. I felt special that if he, indeed, were drafted, he'd enter the league a committed man, giving us the opportunity to build upon our foundation as a team.

Draft day was upon us, and he wasn't selected the first day, which was on a Saturday. That Sunday, I did my normal routine and went to church. I wasn't going to sit around watching the draft on television and not give God His praise. If anything, I felt the news would be better accepted in the House of the Lord. I was in church thanking God for all He had done in our lives when my fiancé showed up, sat down next to me, and whispered, “We are going to Tennessee.” I’m not sure if he would have come to church that day if he hadn’t gotten drafted, but I was glad to have him with me in service.

In the months that followed, we said our “I dos,” exchanged vows, and headed from Detroit, Michigan, to Nashville, Tennessee, where we had no one but each other. We left Michigan with my parents’ blessing and belief that I would be protected, respected, and cherished in my new role as wife. I was fortunate enough to have my job transferred, so we were both on track to manifest our dreams and build a solid foundation together. Now, let me say this: a 4th round draft pick in 1997 did not equate to a huge NFL contract. We had to be smart, live modestly, and plan with our money. I was extremely happy that my background was in the field of finance. I continued to work and handle our family’s finances. I surrounded us with a team of capable people to ensure we didn’t make the common financial mistakes associated with athletes.

So much took place after the move. My husband performed well in the NFL as a wide receiver, and the contracts and signing bonuses increased. With more money and notoriety, life was evolving, and time began to test the layers of our foundation and the values that lay within our hearts.

Different people have different meanings for the word *value*. Let's be clear for the sake of this life lesson. *Value*, as defined by Webster's Dictionary, is "the regard that something is held to deserve; the importance, worth or usefulness of something; one's judgment of what is important."

I always knew my value and what I brought to the marriage. I knew I was educated, honest, hardworking, dedicated, a loyal wife, and a great mom, among many other things. My issue wasn't knowing my own value. My issue was looking for him to acknowledge it the way he did when we were dating. It was as if my soul were screaming, "*Do you still see me? Do you still recognize the love in my heart for you?*" I wanted him to validate what I already knew. And in my quest for validation, I began to lose my focus of me. I lost focus of what was important because I was too busy wanting him to see ME as valuable. He saw the value *in* me, but he didn't see the value *of* me.

Let me explain in case there is another who has or is experiencing the same thing. During our fifteen years of marriage, he stopped saying the important things that were essential to my self-confidence. I don't recall him ever telling me what he loved about me, yet I knew exactly what it was about him that I loved. It seems odd now. But that's the honest truth. So, there I was in a relationship and marriage to a man that claimed he loved me, yet I wasn't exactly sure what he loved about me. That is a slippery slope for disaster. When someone describes what they love about you, and it goes like this . . . *"I love the way you take care of our children, I love the way you keep the house, and I love how you handle our finances"* . . . that is a big problem. Let me tell you why. Because everything just described is a benefit to him and value for him. Value is not how well one can take care of a spouse's "to-do list."

You have to know your worth. You have to believe you are worth real love and a real commitment. You have to know you are worth being respected, cherished, and adored in all aspects of the marriage. I once read that the quality of relationships is tied to our level of self-worth. You are most important in knowing and acknowledging your self-worth. It's an inside job that starts from within. Stop allowing the epidemic of society's low self-esteem to set the tone for your self-worth.

Do you know your worth? What do you want out of life? What do you want out of love? Think back to the first dream you had of your marriage and what it was like. You have to pinpoint that moment when your life began to shift and you began to lose yourself and forget your worth. Once you locate that point, you can begin to redesign your life and get back to your worth. You're worth your heart's desires. We have to stop allowing our past history and outdated circumstances to keep us tied to broken self-identities that don't seem to elevate us to new levels.

Sometimes, a man will ask you to forget your value without actually saying a word. He'll ask you to let him grow up while he's with you. He wants to neglect the responsibilities of adulthood and remain obsessed with the features of boyhood. He devalues you by not taking responsibility for his choices, his family, his community, and the future generation. You answer him with a "yes" a lot of times just by not speaking your hearts' desires and needs. Then, later, it hits you that he may never grow up on his own and that some changes need to be made.

Please use this chapter to write some things out for yourself so you can begin to take action and reconnect with your true value.

Write a few sentences about how you'd like to be treated by a man.

How would you like your value to be expressed to you?

What is it about him that you value?

What is it about you that he values (in your experience)?

Compromise, but don't settle

"Don't settle for less than you deserve."

~ Author unknown

How many times have we found ourselves in a situation where we made a particular choice and felt terrible afterwards? We were angry with ourselves for giving up so much. This would be a situation where we settled instead of compromising. There is a difference between compromising and settling. We often confuse the two, but they are not similar by any means. A compromise is reaching an agreement by each side making concessions. Settling is reaching that same agreement with only you making the concession! Even when you compromise, there is such a thing as an unhealthy compromise versus a healthy compromise. A healthy compromise doesn't go against your morals and values. We should never compromise our habits or selves in such a manner or we are no longer authentic or thriving.

My marriage was full of compromises. Some were healthy, which is to be expected in a marriage. Some were not so healthy, which should not happen at all. A healthy compromise was when I decided to give up my management position and stay home with our children until they were old enough to speak and express themselves. That was for their safety and the well-being of our family. I have no regrets. I loved my job and had worked very hard to earn my status, but I also understood the importance of priorities, and my family came first.

But then you have the unhealthy compromise. The unhealthy compromise was when I began to do nothing but serve the purpose of my ex-husband and forget about my own. I forgot about my visions and passions that had brought me fulfillment. I began to run his foundation, handle his Reebok and Nike endorsement agreements, deal with his agents, and handle our finances, in addition to raising our two beautiful children. My existence started to reflect my total service to him. I bought into every aspect of his dreams, but mine were being neglected. We had often discussed my passion for fashion and opening up a boutique, but the discussion always led back to timing. It seemed my sole responsibility at the time was to ensure that all he had to do was step on the field and play football. Yes, I did that. I handled everything to keep him focused on his career while mine died within me.

Psychoanalyst Beverly Engel describes this as "Disappearing Woman Syndrome." It is the process by which women lose track of what they believe in, what they stand for, and what makes them happy. I can honestly say I severely suffered from "Disappearing Woman Syndrome." Some may ask, "*Well, how does this go against your morals and values to be considered unhealthy?*" When the attention and devotion to our spouses, responsibilities, distractions, and even children become the priority of our lives, the personal relationship with God begins to suffer. That is unhealthy and can leave us vulnerable.

The unhealthy compromises and vulnerability will eventually lead to settling. I was no longer considering my needs; I was settling for the fact that my passions and desires may never be pursued or fulfilled. Now, please don't misunderstand me—we as wives should most certainly support our husbands in their endeavors but not at the expense of completely losing our identity or completely forfeiting our own dreams and spiritual growth. Support works two ways!

I was settling for less than I deserved, and, without realizing it, that became my norm. Compromising should never be so drastic that you lose your self-identity.

Please take note: there is a difference between compromising *in* a relationship and compromising yourself *for* a relationship. How did I get to that point? How do so many women get to that point?

The life lesson of this chapter is simple: there is a difference between compromising and settling. There is a need for both parties to understand the necessity of compromise, and sacrifice from each is essential for it to work. There are healthy compromises and there are unhealthy compromises. Make sure the compromises you're making are not compromising your life's desires, identity, spiritual growth, or self-respect.

In this section, I want you to take the time to identify the areas where you've settled. By doing this, you are confronting yourself, and that will help you decide if it's time to make a change or adjustment.

List at least three things that you feel are healthy compromises.

List some things that you've settled for and that you know you have to change.

What is your plan of action for change? (Take the first step.)

Pursue your purpose

"There is no greater gift you can give or receive than to honor your calling. It's why you were born. And how you become most truly alive."

~ Oprah Winfrey

I COULDN'T AGREE MORE with this quote. We all, indeed, have a purpose and a responsibility to find and follow that purpose. It is why we were created and contributes to our feeling of being alive. What happens in marriage, at times, is that duty replaces purpose. We get so caught up in our duties as spouses and even parents that we forget about our duty to pursue our purpose.

As women, we are natural caretakers and givers, so it's so easy to fall into the role of assistant, manager, mommy, nanny, chef, maid, or any of the many titles we assume as supportive wives. We do it naturally, but if we don't do anything to seek out our own purpose, we become empty and unfulfilled. This can lead to feelings of disappointment and unfulfillment. The purpose of the one life that we have been given is to pursue purpose. We are meant to carry out our visions in life. Many of us don't because our dreams are sidetracked by circumstances and we just can't seem to get back on the right track. In order to do this, we must not only change our circumstances but also our mindset. Finding happiness and pursuing purpose starts within self! It's okay to slow down and take a rest, but you know the saying: "we cannot quit." So, while the circumstances of life have knocked the wind out of us at times, we must take a deep breath and prepare to get up and get busy pursuing our purpose.

In a perfect world, you should have the support of your spouse in whatever your endeavors may be. But if you don't, you cannot give up. Ideally, the two of you should be in one accord to be successful in fulfilling your purpose. Sit down and have the real conversations needed with your spouse about what you want to do in life; the two of you should come to terms on how it will all be accomplished. It may not be easy, and sacrifices may need to be made, but if you care about the wellbeing of each other and the marriage, then the two of you will do everything in your powers to support the pursuit of your individual and joint purposes. Spouses must understand that the type of support that is needed encompasses a combination of emotional, physical, spiritual, and financial. All of these are keys to success and make a difference in the process. Often times, we are afforded one without the others.

One of my biggest mistakes was to delay my purpose to service the needs of my husband's passion. I put his passions before my purpose. Don't get me wrong, I loved being a supportive wife, but I needed to find a balance between serving his passions and pursuing my purpose. Because he had the bigger job and the bigger purpose, so it seemed, I took a backseat and put my purpose on an indefinite hold. Experience is the best teacher, so allow me to teach you from my experience. To give up on your purpose is a huge mistake. Yes, take care of the home, but find a way to balance what you have to do at home with what you need to do outside of the home. You must have an identity in the relationship. Remember, the two shall become one. That means that you're intended to be your own person with your own purpose joining together with your husband. Don't lose yourself. Don't forget who you are and what purpose you were intended to serve. Don't get so caught up in his life that you overlook your own.

I gave up my career to raise our family and assist in spearheading his endeavors. When the time came for me to resume my purpose, I was stunned. Why? Because years of serving on committees, helping with foundations, reviewing agreements, and watching over our funds didn't seem to make a bit of difference in helping me to garner the spiritual, emotional, and physical support I needed. That was heartbreaking. What happened to the saying, "treat others as you would have them to treat you"? I had done my part for the team and was ready for the team to do its part for me. Well, that just wasn't the case. So, there I was, ready to identify my purpose with little-to-no emotional, spiritual, or physical support from my spouse. I felt I was starting my journey alone. Everyone needs a cheerleader, and we would think that would be our spouse. I had played the role so well that there was very little doubt in my mind that it would be returned. I guess there is a lesson to be learned within this lesson: never assume anything! I assumed if I wholeheartedly supported my husband, when the time came, he would wholeheartedly support me.

In any event, it was time to pursue my purpose. Our children were older, and I needed to start pursuing those things that were important to me. While the journey to fulfill purpose is not always easy, it is always worth it. I am thankful that my life lessons are a part of my purpose and my journey to share with the world. Yes, I should have gotten started sooner, but, as the saying goes, "better late than never." I am fulfilling my purpose-driven life and would like to encourage you to do the same. If you have stopped pursuing your purpose or have allowed duty to replace it, make an adjustment.

Sit down today and write out your passions and your purpose. Then, write out your plans. Think about the balance you will need to find to be successful in the home and outside of the home in your passion work. If there is a conversation that needs to be had, then start thinking about how you will approach it. Don't neglect yourself. Don't forget what you love, and don't put all of your passions on the back burner forever. There is something that can bring you extra joy and fulfillment, and you deserve to have that. You have to believe that, and you have to move toward it. Don't give up on your purpose. Pursue it relentlessly. You deserve to have it all.

Make a list of some of your passions.

What do you believe to be your purpose?

What is your plan of action to pursue your purpose?

What would you like your mate to do to support your purpose? (Share this with your spouse.)

Love isn't for sale

"There is a difference in leasing
your affections and buying
into your expectations."
- Life Lessons of Marci Mason

"Love isn't for sale" is one of the hardest life lessons to communicate and discuss mostly because our society holds such high regard to money, status, and material things. This lesson will be hard because there are more offenses than we care to talk about. And there are times when society doesn't take this life lesson to heart because the bigger picture generally sides with money and not ethics. I know that sounds strange, but, as we go deeper, you will understand better. With money, you can buy so many things that *make* you happy, but, unfortunately, you can't buy the fundamentals of life or love to *keep* you happy. This is the life lesson that we will really need in order to be truthful and look deep within our own hearts for answers, methods of change, and a progressive plan to move forward.

I have decided to tackle this life lesson from a different perspective—discussing the effects of those looking to sell their love to those who are already committed. If we are honest with each other, and ourselves, we will admit that this is a downright touchy subject to address, but somebody has to do it. If you are unfortunate enough to have to deal with someone who doesn't understand that love isn't for sale, then you know this experience comes with some pain, resentment, and downright shame. See, I told you this would be tough to talk about. Let's explore and discuss this issue more in depth to recognize it, address it, and move pass it, as painful as it may be.

This life lesson was easier to tackle when women thought twice about being a home wrecker or enabling a cheater. In past times, there was not a spotlight or a reward of "15 minutes of fame." Wives didn't have to be publicly humiliated from the antics of those looking to sell their love or, to put it more practically, lease their affections.

The emotional pain, the aftereffects to the relationship, and the damage put forth from these situations are worth the discussion. If you are a woman and have dealt with another woman seeking the affections of your man, willing to lease out her love in hopes of the final purchase, then you may be all too familiar with this circumstance. You are fed up with having to deal with the additional emotional obstruction to your marriage. You want to yell from the top of your lungs, "*Just because my husband will sleep with you doesn't mean he will marry you!*" You wish you could pound into their heads and hearts that "*just because he is leasing your affections doesn't mean he is buying into your expectations.*" Well, we just said it. And, honestly, it feels good.

And these WOTS (Women On The Side) have the nerve to have an attitude with the WIFE! This is where we as women have to really hold it together and apply the lessons of this chapter. We have to collect all of our faith and rely on it to keep us strong enough to not lay hands! Oh, come on now, any woman who has ever dealt with infidelity truly understands the term "self-control." When you get the inkling about this, you want to throw out all class, take off the earrings, and grab "some Vaseline," as Jill Scott so passionately sings in one of her songs. Our flesh wants to conveniently tuck away our spiritual guidance, the moral compass, and take it straight to the streets with both him and her. WOTS who knowingly become involved with married men are the worst. There is no shame in their game, and they come to seek, steal, and destroy. When my husband first entered the league, a very good friend once joked about having a t-shirt made that stated: "WIVES, not WOTS!" While it didn't mean much at the time, I never forgot the term *WOTS*.

Once you are certain that your spouse is committing adultery, you have some very serious decisions to make. These are decisions that cannot be made by anyone but you. Each situation is different, and each outcome is unique to the couple. Only discuss your situation with people you trust, and please make sure they are of good character. The Bible tells us to seek wise counsel, not just counsel. And as hard as it may be for you, because we know WOTS tend to provoke, please don't allow anyone to take you out of your character and force you to do anything you may later regret. It's your life that they want; remember that, and react accordingly.

Also, understand that infidelity doesn't always have to equate to divorce. If two people are willing to work through the emotional pain of an affair, the marriage can be saved. The key is that it takes two people willing to forgive, change some behaviors, and work toward a new path. This calls for true forgiveness and real work on the behalf of both parties. You have to deal with the shame, guilt, and root cause of the situation.

If two people truly love each other and want it to work, they can put the past behind them. They can put their lives and love back into perspective and begin to rebuild on the solid foundation that was started in Chapter One.

On the other side of that situation, if he is not willing to change his behavior and respect the commitment, you also have some serious decisions to make . No one should stay simply because they have become comfortable with a lifestyle. You have to ask yourself if you want to be respected, or is it enough simply to stay comfortable? Research has shown that people would prefer to stay in bad situations because they are comfortable, know what to expect, and can plan accordingly rather than leave and face the unexpected. It sounds strange, but, as I think about it, I see some truth. It is always easier to deal with what we know than to face what we don't. Almost every motivational speech I have taken to heart confirms that elevation means moving beyond your comfort zone. So, if you stay for comfort, please understand exactly what that means to your future and your purpose.

Who do you consider to be WISE enough to counsel you and why?

Weigh the pros and cons of your situation. Make an extensive list. Thoroughly consider it. List the pros first.

Now, list the cons.

Reality vs. Perception

"Don't be so quick to defend your perception without even considering your reality."

~ LIFE LESSONS OF MARCI MASON

WHO WE ARE versus who people *think* we are can be vastly different at times, to say the least. We confuse our own perceptions with reality, so it's easy to accept when others do the same. Reality vs. perception is a great discussion to have because it forces us to take a good look at our personal situations. It then puts us in the mindset to be honest with ourselves about the match up of what is perceived and what is real.

Our world is built on perceptions. Young adults perceive from famous artists that they are performing their reality. The perception of women in media has many of us confused about the reality of what beauty really looks like. Oh, and how many times have we met someone who we perceive as one way but find out in reality they are completely different? I use these examples to prove the point that "reality versus perception" is an ongoing life lesson for many of us that needs to be acknowledged and addressed. We especially have to begin to acknowledge the perceptions in our lives that are harmful to our reality.

As women, we often try to convince others, and ourselves, that we don't care what others think of us. And the truth is . . . we actually care quite a bit. If none of us truly cared what others thought, we would be so much more transparent in our digressions in life. When the perception is bad or displeasing, we do all we can to change it. But when the perception is good, we do all we can to protect it, even when that perception is harmful to our reality.

Let's discuss some of the reasons why we do it. Aren't we sometimes protecting our family image? When we weigh the pros and cons of exposing perception, we take into account more than just ourselves. Until the shoe is on your foot, it's very hard to determine why people do what they do. Perhaps we are protecting our reputation or self-respect. Let's be honest: we live in a world where people judge us for our situations and circumstances.

And we live in a world where people rely on such judgment to make it easier for them to create their own perceptions of us. And perhaps we won't address the deception of perception because we were deceived and not yet ready to confess to having been a victim of manipulation.

When you see past articles about my family, we were often described as a loving, Christian family. Some have even labeled us a good example of what family looks like. We have graced covers and taken part in many family-oriented events because of the perception of our lives. I was made a promise that family was very important and nothing would ever come between that. What life experiences have taught me is that even in our own lives we must learn to distinguish the manipulation of perception from reality. Yes, I said, "manipulation," because that's what it really boils down to for many. When reality did hit me, I was devastated, to say the least, but without those experiences, I would have nothing to share with you to propel your growth.

You see, some of my perceptions were created a long time ago and forced into my reality. Nevertheless, when the two collided, life lessons were learned. There was the perception that the forest green Toyota from our first date belonged to him, BUT the reality was that it belonged to his ex-girlfriend. There was the perception that my husband adored his family. Literally before every game, he publicly wrote my name and the names of our children along with his favorite scripture on his cleats, BUT the reality was that he was cheating, jeopardizing the future of our entire foundation. There was the perception that he needed massages to recover from the pain of the game, BUT the reality, I later learned, was that his certified masseuse was one of his mistresses. I think the biggest perception was his openly communicated commitment to the children and me (which could be heard in many interviews), BUT the reality was that the commitment sounded good for the public image.

We all deserve the truth and to live a truthful life. We all deserve for our perception to match our reality, and when it doesn't, we MUST make changes. I am not suggesting anyone leave his or her marriage, but I am suggesting that behavioral changes must take place for the marriage to be saved. My realities may be different than yours, but all of them are equally important. Perceptions can be deceiving, and you do not have to put up with them, especially when they are harmful to your reality.

Sit down and confront the reality of your perceptions. Make your spouse a part of the discussion. If your spouse isn't willing to work on your relationship, then your reality is that he doesn't really love you enough to make the necessary changes. A man works for what he wants. You have to face the reality of the situation at some point. We run from reality hoping that it will just change on its own. That's not going to happen. It takes work. I don't think any woman is exempt from these issues. I believe that every woman has to deal with perceptions and the manipulation of perceptions at some point in her life.

I challenge you today to live truthfully. I challenge you to speak up if your reality doesn't match the perception. I challenge you to ask for a sit down with your spouse and talk like mature adults. Try to work things out and move toward a healthy relationship together. If he refuses to change, then you might want to consider all of your options. You don't have to live a lie or continue to be manipulated. You're not getting any younger, so if the situation isn't getting any better, then some changes must be made. I wish I had figured out sooner that even my perceptions were not my reality. I prayed. I tried counseling. I called upon some of his closest friends and spiritual leaders. I did all I knew to do to bridge the two. Eventually, it became too much to carry. You know what you need to change. Be committed to making those changes.

Write a short paragraph about what you desire the reality of your relationship to be.

Do you recognize perceptions that do not match up to your reality? List them.

If so, what is your plan of action? Discuss with your mate.

The breaking point

"Everyone has a breaking point, know yours!"

~ Life Lessons of Marci Mason

We each have a breaking point. I think we fear that point. It's the point of no return. It's the point when it feels like failure is confirmed. We feel like we've wasted so much time and we've fought so hard, but yet we are still about to lose what seems to be everything. Not every relationship has a breaking point because some relationships are meant to be, but if it's *not* meant to be, we have to realize it to start moving beyond the pain.

I remember the breaking point in my relationship, and I bet it wasn't much different from what others have experienced. I think many of us know what it looks and feels like. For me, the breaking point was when my kids began to experience the pain with me. When they began to witness things they had never seen or things I never intended for them to see. We faithfully spent Friday nights as "Family Night" by doing an activity with our children. Over time, this began to cease, and our kids noticed. They noticed their dad didn't really spend much time at home with us anymore.

Why did the kids have to suffer because of what we were going through? I would sometimes scream and shout at their father as if the volume of my voice could change the circumstances of my heart. I began to act differently. I was going his through emails, checking his phone, and combing through his social media accounts as if I were a private detective. I was changing as a person. More importantly, my kids are my world, and when they hurt, I hurt even more. That was another sign that the end was near. I honestly felt I no longer knew this man.

My heart was broken, and I had fallen out of "like" with him. I didn't trust him anymore. I loved him, but I didn't like him. I didn't want to be intimate with him because I felt my health was at risk. I am diabetic, and sickness affects my body differently than it does others. Yes, I had reached my breaking point. When fleshly desires are so powerful that all logic is absent, it is time to reconsider life choices. Why would anyone take such risks and include me in the equation?

When you know it's time to let it go, you have to prepare for it spiritually, mentally, physically, emotionally, and financially. I was able to think it through and prepare my exit plan. My children were involved, so there was a lot I had to weigh. I had to think about where we would live, where they would go to school, and how I would make a living for them. I needed a good attorney to learn about my rights. The laws are different in each state. It is important to educate yourself to ensure your best interests are considered. I had to read and study about divorce and how things would play out in a manner that was fair for all parties involved, including me. I didn't want my divorce to be a public spectacle. It took a lot of time gearing up my heart and mind to leave. It's not easy to let go after you've invested so much of yourself to make it work. And I had invested all that I had to invest.

To make matters worse, my husband didn't want a divorce and said he would contest it. He said he didn't want to lose his family. How ironic! You'd think that he'd be ready to let go so he could live his life the way he wanted to and not have to answer to anyone about his wrongdoings. But he gave some resistance. Maybe it's a "man thing" because I've heard of several other men doing the same thing. I had to move forward with the divorce even if he wasn't willing to agree to it. It was no longer just about him. At this point, it also became about the kids and myself. I had to do what was best for us. I moved forward with the divorce. It was one of the hardest things I've done in my entire life!

It really hit me hard once I accepted it was really over. I could feel my heart crumbling. It was like the air had been knocked completely out of me. I felt empty and lost. It hurt very badly. I was hurting more than I'd ever hurt before; my soul was in critical condition. I thought that I would be married to this man forever. No one could have prepared me for the deception that I encountered. My parents are still together, and our family holds marriage in high regard. I never thought my marriage would end in divorce.

But it was bigger than I was. I was also thinking about my kids. My heart hurt for them. I didn't want my kids to have to go through this so young in their lives. I didn't want to be a single mom or a statistic. I wanted my kids to be raised in a home with their father. I wanted my daughter to be able to come home to her father and get advice that only a father can give. I wanted her to have that security of a father figure in the home. I wanted my son to be able to see a real man in the home and be raised by a man. I wanted him to be able to get the lessons that every young man needs from his father. I wanted him to be able to watch his father shave and fix things around the house. I wanted him to grow up watching a man so it would help him become a man.

Now, I had to figure out how I would pull things together. I had to figure out how I would pull myself up and keep going. I put so much into my marriage. I sacrificed so much of my life. I sacrificed my emotional wellbeing. I sacrificed my passions and my purpose. I sacrificed my time. I sacrificed my body and brought two beautiful children into the world with the promise we would raise them together. I gave up my last name. I left my family and hometown to be with my husband. I became a full-time mother and wife. Only to have it all end because of selfish choices and temporary pleasures.

Divorce is one of the hardest things a person can go through, but, sometimes, it's necessary. I know there are people who feel like we should stick it out no matter what, but bad behavior without change is reason for divorce. You have to look out for yourself first. This may sound selfish, but, in reality, it's not. What good are you to your kids if you're no good to yourself? I hate that things had to turn out the way they did, but I'm thankful that God gave me the strength to get through it.

You have to know your breaking point. Don't risk pushing beyond your breaking point because you might not be able to recover whole again. We see this happening to so many people; they push beyond their breaking point, and they end up scarred and bitter. The pain gets so bad that it torments the heart and begins to regulate the mind. Let's not go from relationship to relationship, sabotaging them because of the pain of the past. We must refuse to live that way. I personally refuse to go into another relationship broken and hurt. I'm working on myself and making sure that I'm whole. I've been through enough, and I have to heal and prepare for what's to come. If you are in this situation, you owe it to yourself to do the same thing. Become whole again.

There is healing after a divorce or bad breakup. It will take some time, but you have to push beyond the pain. You have to be willing to go from day to day with the faith that it will get better. The pain doesn't end because the marriage or relationship ends. Prepare yourself for situations of tests, conversations of mess, and confirmations of more stress. Just remember, you have come to your breaking point, and you cannot turn back now! Take some time and identify your breaking point.

What do you think is your breaking point?

Have you reached your breaking point? If so, how did you identify it?

What are some realistic goals for change?

How soon can you begin to implement these changes? (Step 1)

Know your pretty-point

"You don't need other people to value you. You're already valuable."

~ Life Lessons of Marci Mason

LET'S BE REAL: after a divorce or major break up, our confidence can be shattered. What we do know is we can't change the past no matter how long or hard we hold on to it. Therefore, it is best to let it go and move forward. And this starts with renewing self. It begins with rebuilding your confidence in self and in life. This task starts in the mind. Actions are manifested from thought. We must change or refocus our thoughts. We have to regain our confidence and be reminded of our pretty-point.

I am not talking about some physical attribute that defines our beauty; it's so much deeper than that. I am speaking of the point in our minds and hearts that believes we are valuable, the place we all need to be reminded of when we look to others for confirmation. Think of the times when you asked yourself, "*What is it about me that is not good enough for him?*" "*Nothing about you*" is the answer. We must not blame ourselves for the poor decisions of others. But we must hold ourselves accountable for renewing a spirit within us to move forward into a space that's healthy.

I am not suggesting that this is easy. It takes time, energy, and perseverance. This is a new point in life we must overcome and adjust to in the process. For me, personally, I experienced things I never imagined. I was confronted with situations that questioned my self-worth. I had honored my wedding vows, yet my friendships and relationships were being tested. People that I thought were true friends were more concerned with maintaining his acknowledgment rather than our friendships; not because they were such great friends with him, but because they felt there was something to gain in being a friend of his. I didn't realize when going through a divorce that you don't lose just your spouse, you may also lose some friends. It was my first experience at divorce, so I honestly didn't know. The ability to have a ball signed or have him make an appearance at an event suddenly became more important than the years of time we shared. "*Wow*" was all I could say. If, at this point, you don't know your pretty-point, you most certainly will begin to question everything you do know about yourself.

It is also very important that you do the things that make you feel good about yourself on the outside as well as the inside. This may sound elementary, but when you get stuck in pain, neglecting self becomes easy. It may be when you get your hair done. It may be when you exercise. It may be when you get a massage or get your nails done. It could be a combination of them all. Whatever the case, know what makes you feel good about yourself and be willing to do that over and over again. It's during these tough times that you learn who your true friends really are and who was around only for the benefits.

You have to be able to validate yourself. You have to create a pretty-point system that validates you for you. This should be a combination of things that you can do to lift your spirits and feel good about yourself. I want you to start thinking about your pretty-point so you can write it down later. After you write it down, you'll be able to etch it into your mind and ensure that the process is not forgotten. Again, it's much more than your appearance. It's your wellbeing. It's your physical and spiritual health. It's your emotional state.

If it takes a man to validate you, then you'll always need him. So, what happens when he doesn't validate you? You feel worthless. It's not a good feeling to have to depend on someone else for your worth. If you get to that point, then you have surrendered your control of your life to this person. Never give your power to someone else. You must have power of your own life, even in circumstances beyond your control.

If, for any reason, you are at this point and cannot find your way back to a healthy pretty-point, please don't hesitate to get outside help. So many of us look down on therapy and allow our issues to become more complex. It does not have to be this way.

Think about your weaknesses right now. Think about where you're lacking in your happiness. Are you at your pretty-point on the inside and out? What do you need to do to get there? Are you willing to work for it? Set a schedule for yourself to do the things you need to do daily to reach your pretty-point. Become the CEO of your life and make yourself a priority. You need you! If you're broken down, then how can you help anyone else? How can you be a positive influence on your children with no positivity in your life? How can you perform your job to the best of your abilities if you can't even look up? You have to take care of you before you can take care of anyone or anything else.

This is a realization that we all must come to in order to fix our situations after our circumstances. When I opened my eyes to the fact that I had complete control over my own happiness, it was then that things began to change for me. It wasn't a cakewalk. It was hard, but I knew I could do it. If I can do it, then I'm convinced that you can, too. Don't lie to yourself. Don't tell yourself that you're whole and healthy if you know you're not. Don't let your outer appearance fool you into thinking that you're pretty on the inside, yet your heart is bleeding. You have to look within first. Fix the inside, then prepare the outside to match.

I'd like for you to take some time and think about all that we have discussed in this chapter. I know talking about pretty-points after such a disaster seems a bit strange, but if you have been through the pain discussed, you understand the point where you were and the point to where you need to get back. Don't fall out of love with yourself just because someone else didn't love you the way you deserve to be loved.

What things can you do to reach your pretty-point on the inside and out?

When was the last time you were at your pretty-point?

The next time you're not feeling at your pretty-point, what will you do?

Parenting through the pain

"Don't burden your children
with situations they can't control,
and don't ask your children to
deal with adult issues."

- Dr. Phil

ALONG WITH TAKING care of yourself, parenting has to be a priority. I had to come to the realization that this was bigger than he and I. It was no longer about us but about the two children that needed guidance despite any emotional circumstances that were present. Unfortunately, we don't get to put parenting on hold while the adults sort out their life decisions and mistakes. It amazes me how quickly the world just wants us to get over it. Well, it's just not that easy. Women are creatures of love, and we don't just leave 15 years of marriage and get over it without a healing process. Such an experience comes with some emotional pain and adjustment. There were so many days when I didn't want to get out of bed. I can admit that I just wanted to sit in a dark room, not eat, and cry my heart out. I wanted explanations. I wanted to understand. I wanted to know how we ended up there. I couldn't really see when the pain would subside. I couldn't believe that this was a part of my destination.

My kids are my world, and it's such a pleasure to have them. I feel honored to be a mother because it wasn't an easy road for me. I'm an insulin-dependent diabetic, so my pregnancies were very high risk. During my first pregnancy, I developed cysts on one of my ovaries that were extracting nutrients needed by the baby. Surgery was required. The doctor had to move my daughter to one side and proceed to remove my left ovary. That was a scary time, but we got through it. So, when I had my son, it was surely a blessing as I only had one ovary when I conceived him, which is rare. Complications like those made having children so special. I don't take their little lives for granted in the least. I feel blessed and loved by God to have been given the opportunity to be called "mother."

It has always been a practice between us that our children come first. This life lesson comes on the heels of witnessing that parenting does change in the midst of divorce. There are new situations to address, new circumstances that arise, and lots of emotions that affect your children . This was all new to me and some of the circumstances and situations honestly just caught me off guard.

It's hard enough trying to love yourself when you're broken. When you don't feel like loving yourself, it's even harder to love someone else. I didn't have the energy for love for a little while. If I may be honest, I was so drained from the aftermath of my marriage that it took everything in me to put up the front of happy mommy for my children. When they went to school, I went back to bed until it was time for them to return home. Then, I was up again for their sakes. I knew it was important that they see me at least appearing normal. It wasn't unusual for my mother to visit and help out. She is very close to my children, and I needed her more than ever! She came to visit for a couple of weeks, and she was our rock. She saw me caring for them but not caring for myself. I continued in my routine of caring for them and returning back to bed. Then, one day, she came to me, and she said something that shook my spirit. She said, "*Your kids need your mind, body, and soul in its healthiest form!*" She explained that I was going through the motions of life but not living. I was not taking care of me the way I needed to in order to be healthy and whole for them. That pierced my spirit. Sometimes, when we are not at our best, we do need others to be painfully honest to help us become better.

I had a really good friend who lived completely across town, and she would show up at my door with food. Generally, it was chicken and some rolls. It took all I had to just drag myself out of bed to answer the door. I wanted to sleep until my children returned from school. But she wasn't the type of friend who would let me do that; I would need to answer the door. She would always say the same thing to me: "*I was in the neighborhood and thought you might be hungry.*" I wasn't eating, and my friend knew it. She'd kindly remind me that I could eat the chicken and rolls or I could sip them through a straw. Considering I knew she was never really just in the neighborhood and had driven across town to bring me that food, I believed she just might shovel it down my throat. Thank goodness for family and friends who care. I guess thinking about this and hearing the words spoken from my mother's heart were the confirmations I needed to regroup, refocus, and reconstruct my wholeness. I went into deep prayer, propelled plans of action, and began my journey to move beyond the pain and become whole again. I poured my all into them, and I learned how to heal and how to love again in spite of my circumstances. I really had no choice. Being diabetic, I had to get better for my own sake as well. My parents, my doctor, and my good friend really stayed on my case, and they pushed me to get back up and to stay up.

The truth of this life lesson is that no matter how difficult it is, we can't stop being productive parents. I became a single mom. I suddenly felt that I alone had to care for and make decisions about my children. I didn't have the freedom to show up or not. My every decision took my children into account. I wish I could say that about all parties involved.

The things that women have to deal with after divorce can be downright overbearing at times. As the custodial parent, the responsibilities lie upon you. If the other parent is unavailable for whatever reason, you simply have to shift things around and make life work. The children shouldn't suffer.

Oh, and let's not forget to discuss the effects of parenting when one or both parties are ready to introduce new mates. While this is all new to me, I most certainly feel there should be a protocol that considers the well-being of the children. We have a right to be concerned about who is actively participating in the lives of our children and the influence they bring. Now, I have made a personal decision that until I meet someone that I believe will be a potential marriage partner, my children will not be involved. They are kids; I do not want to plant any seeds that it is okay to play house when I am trying to teach them the responsibility of laying a solid foundation for their future. Nor do I want to burden them with situations beyond their control. Call me old-fashioned, but I want to lead them by example.

Wouldn't life be grand if it were understood there is a certain level of respect that should come from being the mother of your children and your wife of 15 years? It is hard enough navigating through the pain of the circumstances without the additional stresses of "new girlfriend syndrome." You know that syndrome where they think they know him better than you, and what he did to you would never happen to them, and now they want to co-parent your children? We as single moms have enough to worry about. Our children are most important. So, ladies, this is where we have to get up the strength to bypass the BS and concentrate solely on the children. It isn't easy, but we have to find a compromise and do our very best to communicate with all parties to ensure our children's needs are priority. We have to set boundaries to help girlfriends understand their roles in our children's lives. We have to help them understand that their temporary decisions could cause permanent consequences in the lives of our children. Children aren't pawns in a game where we can play with their lives or futures. When starting over, at times, this fact gets lost.

Just because it is best for the ex does not mean it equates to being best for our children. As selfless parents, we must consider and talk through these situations. The choices of the other parent may clearly not be the right choices for our children. Don't be afraid to have the discussion; these are your children, too. I know firsthand this may be hard. But it has to be done. The woman is generally accused of being caught up in feelings that many times don't exist; the truth is we are generally looking out for the best interest of our children. I am sorry to announce that we are not all jealous, scorned divorcées; we simply want to ensure our children are considered and treated accordingly. Why is that so hard to comprehend? Ladies, we must stop allowing others to make us feel as if being good mothers doesn't include questioning the judgment and decisions of the other parent. Now, please don't misunderstand me, children should not be used as pawns for revenge. I am sincerely speaking to the well-being of the children.

There may even need to be counseling in place to ensure all the questions and concerns of the children can be addressed. Whatever is needed to ensure their stability, parents need to get it done.

What I did learn through this experience is children have thoughts and feelings about circumstances, too. As adults, we often forget we must lead by example; our children are watching. This life lesson could go on and on as there are so many dynamics in parenting through the pain. What's most important is that regardless of what you may be experiencing as a result of the decisions made, you must make sure the children are receiving proper care. Prepare yourself to deal with their questions and feelings about the situation, and please don't ever ignore them and just expect them to accept the circumstances and bounce back. They aren't responsible for the situation that affects them. My daughter developed breathing problems during our transition. Doctors couldn't find anything wrong. Tests revealed her lungs were fine, and it was concluded that this was a result of anxiety from the breakdown of our family and, ultimately, the divorce.

One day, your kids will look back over their lives, and they will either see your strength through the struggle or they will see your failure of the struggle. It is not easy to parent through the pain, but it is possible. It's that possibility that we need to grab and hang on to.

It was especially important for me to pour additional efforts, resources, and prayer into my son's life during this transition. What parent doesn't want the best for their children? I do not want him making the same mistakes as the generations that came before him. My family constantly reminds me that thoughts are powerful, so

I am Power Thinking over his life. I declare and decree that he shall be a man of character and integrity. The family foundation starts with the man, and he shall one day positively contribute to his own family and foundation. As his mother, I will never stop praying over his life, his future, and his well-being.

Parent through the pain, and I'm willing to bet that you will get stronger. Will yourself to stay focused on the future of your children. There will be trying times and even some trying people when it comes to the decisions of your children. Ignore the foolishness, and stay the course to guide them effectively. Stay in the fight because if there is any fight worth fighting, this is it.

What's your biggest parenting struggle right now?

What can you do to make that struggle easier on yourself?

Do you talk to your children about issues that are important to them?

Not everything you lose is a loss

"Gain strength through adversity!"
- James A. Murphy

THERE IS ALWAYS a purpose in God's plan for your life. We have to go through some things to get to where God wants us to be. It's the mistakes and the pain that add character to this journey we call "life." It's been said that we have to endure the tough times to get the tough lessons. I've always heard people say, "*The greater the test, the greater the testimony.*" I have found this to be true in my life.

For a while, I was looking at my marriage as a loss. I had lost time, track of my career, respect for the relationship, and my family. But God began to show me all the things that He had saved! And I began to see that there is no message without a mess. There is no glory without a story. And not everything you lose is a loss!

I began to change the way I looked at things. I began to open my eyes and see my situation in a different light. I have to be honest and give some credit to Bishop T.D. Jakes. I listened to many sermons that helped me begin to realize that what I lost wasn't love. You see, real love doesn't hurt but, instead, helps to heal. This realization helped me to put the relationship in perspective and realize that I hadn't really lost as much as I thought. In fact, I had gained so much more. I gained a lot of wisdom. I gained a lot of clarity. I gained two beautiful children. I gained a lot of experience and knowledge about selfless versus selfish. I gained my independence to pursue my purpose. I gained a second chance to find true love that understands commitment and respect. And, most importantly, I gained the opportunity to live a fulfilling life of love.

I had to take everything I'd gone through and move it into my purpose. I had to start living the purpose-driven life God intended me to live. Sometimes, it's those tough life experiences that help us blossom into a new season. I realized that my divorce was the influential factor that pushed me into my season. I was holding back while in my marriage because I didn't have the support of anyone pushing me forward.

If you have heard the saying "Let Go and Let God," it is true. I've started living again. I'm raising my children, and they are growing into beautiful souls. I'm running my company, Marci Mason Media, LLC, and we are on the verge of some big things. I'm living my purpose and my passion. I'm gearing up to start giving back again through my work with the American Diabetes Association, a cause dear to my heart. I am now doing all I can to speak into the lives of other women through my experience. I shared things with you that I never dreamed I'd have to ever deal with, let alone write about. These are things that we as women experience, and rather than hide in shame, we need to discuss and find ways to collectively move beyond.

This is what life is about: *purpose.* You have to look over all the pain that you've endured, and you have to draw a lesson from it. Identify the lessons, then use them to better yourself and help others. In my life experiences, I've seen too many people get hurt and stay hurt. They go through something tough and never bounce back from it. Please don't relish in the sob story, but begin to create a glory story! Allow other people to look at you and be inspired by all that you've overcome.

We all have a purpose, and we have to walk in it. Take the time to do one last exercise with me. I want you to look over your life and identify all the times you've lost something or someone. Then, after you identify those times you've lost something, I want you to identify what you can learn from them. It's important that you change the way you view the things that have happened to you. If you can change the way you see a circumstance, then you will become more confident that you can change from it. Please know that no matter how deep the pain gets, you can truly move beyond it!

List the things you've lost.	*List the lesson(s) you've learned.*

It is my prayer that from this exercise alone you see that not everything you lose is a loss, especially if you learned from it. Move forward with the intent to learn, grow, and change. Use your pain to birth your purpose.

Final thoughts

OUR TIME TOGETHER has come to an end, but I wanted to leave you with some final thoughts. It is always my intent to leave any situation with positive energy and motivational instruction to move forward. My transition was not easy, but I don't want you to feel sorry for me. I want you to see my trials and tribulations and use them to help you know you, too, can move beyond the pain and into your purpose.

Life may not turn out as we thought, but we still have to make the very best of it. We can't give up and get stuck in our situations. At times, we simply have to regroup, reload, and relaunch our lives. We have to take a step back and figure some things out. What we can't do is sit around in an extended pity party. That serves no purpose to anyone.

Yes, it's easier said than done, but you can do it! So, ladies, don't worry about what it all looks like; take the first step toward a new and refined you. Allow this experience to make you better, not bitter. It didn't go as planned, and it most certainly didn't end the way you expected, but it's okay. Life goes on, and you will make it through.

It is time to take back a firm grasp of our power. Losing power over self is harmful to our self-esteem and future happiness. This is why we must lose the fear and take the necessary actions to gain back our self-respect and power to live our lives. We are no longer the victim of our circumstances but the victor of our second chances. Don't be paralyzed by fear but empowered by fearlessness. We know overcoming fear doesn't mean it goes away forever or no longer exists, it simply means we choose to understand it for the emotion that it is and not the driving force of our destiny!

Please understand I'm speaking from true experience. I am not just saying what I think sounds good. I am saying it because I mean it. I have lived through it and come out of it, and you can, too. Well, my days aren't always smooth sailing, I continue to practice each of the life lessons mentioned to elevate my happiness. We all have a purpose for our lives, and, regardless of our circumstances, we have a responsibility to carry out that purpose. Don't let your temporary detours keep you from reaching your final destination!

I hope reading this book has helped you as much as writing it has helped me. I hope that you can look over your life, take the lessons from it, and then find the strength to keep getting better. I know that we all get hurt, but we should all get back up. There is so much more to life than going from pain to pain. We have to embrace our gifts and talents and walk in purpose. We have to be fearless and fabulous. We have to be focused on impacting the world and not just being successful but also significant. If you have children counting on you, be strong for them. There isn't a man in the world worth losing yourself over. If a man can't love you the way you deserve to be loved, then you have to love yourself enough to let him go.

Let me leave you with this. As you lay the solid foundation of life, know your value in a relationship and be prepared to compromise, but don't settle. Always continue to pursue your purpose. Constantly remind yourself and your mate that love isn't for sale, and make certain that your reality matches your perception. If you ever get to your breaking point, please know your pretty-point, and if you must parent through the pain, realize sooner rather than later that not everything you lose is a loss.

About the Author

Marci Mason is a woman who has survived her pain and hopes to encourage and empower others so that they, too, can move beyond the pain. After 15 years of marriage, she was devastated when faced with the reality of a divorce and raising two children alone. She married her best friend and truly believed they would be together for life. We all must come to grips with the fact that plans change in life and we have to adapt to the changes of life. Some change is good, some change is not so good, and some change is just necessary. Marci takes her readers on a short journey of her changes in the hopes that her complicated truths, adverse situations, and new accomplishments can be an inspiration to others so that they can, indeed, move beyond the pain and live a fulfilled life.

For Bookings:
BookMarci@marcimason.com

For General Inquiries:
Info@marcimason.com

To keep up with the latest books & news from Marci, please visit:
www.marcimason.com

Social Media Connections:

Officialmarcimason

@Marcimason

Marcimason

Special Thanks

To my God who has kept me, loved me, and spiritually wiped every tear I've cried. I am ever so grateful to my Lord and Savior.

I would like to thank my Mom for loving me and B and D the way you do. Thanking you for being an example of unselfish love in our lives. You're the woman I admire most in this world. You have always done your best even when, sometimes, the cards were stacked against you with less. You're the strongest woman I know. I am blessed because you're my MOM. For every powerful prayer you prayed for me during the dark days . . . MOMMY, I thank you.

I would like to thank my Dad for your love and support. You got it right before the end of the fight! I love you more and more each and every day. Thank you for every laugh that made my stomach hurt and being the best Granddad B and D could ever have.

I would like to thank my friend Wendy for all of your love and support. For all the late night talk sessions, sleepovers, and threats to make me suck my food through a straw if I wouldn't eat . . . LOL. Thank you for seeing the best in me when it became hard to recognize it for myself. Thank you for always supporting me and pushing me to be better.

I would like to thank Maggie for your love and loyalty to my family. Oh, and for giving birth to my one and only godchild . . . "Papa Bear."

I would like to thank Jay for being my financial gatekeeper over the years. I thank you for all of your advice and appreciate your willingness to share your wisdom. You have always gone over and beyond what the position of financial advisor requires.

I would like to thank Tracy for all of your encouragement, support, and wise counsel! You kept me sane through it all.